AMERICAN COMMUNITIES

We Live in a
STATE CAPITAL

Leslie Beckett

PowerKiDS press.

New York

Published in 2016 by The Rosen Publishing Group, Inc.
29 East 21st Street, New York, NY 10010

First Edition

Editor: Katie Kawa
Book Design: Reann Nye

Photo Credits: Cover, pp. 3–24 (background texture) Evgeny Karandaev/Shutterstock.com; cover, p. 22 Charles Knowles/Shutterstock.com; pp. 5, 24 (capitol) Joseph Sohm/Shutterstock.com; p. 6 Anna Gorin/Moment Open/Getty Images; p. 9 Nagel Photography/Shutterstock.com; p. 10 Dave and Les Jacobs/Blend Images/Getty Images; pp. 13, 14 Otto Kitsinger/AP Images; p. 17 © iStockphoto.com/Mypurgatoryyears; p. 18 (top) KENNY TONG/Shutterstock.com; p. 18 (bottom) aceshot1/Shutterstock.com; p. 21 Cvijun/Shutterstock.com; p. 24 (museum) Semmick Photo/Shutterstock.com.

Cataloging-in-Publication Data

Beckett, Leslie.
We live in a state capital / by Leslie Beckett.
p. cm. — (American communities)
Includes index.
ISBN 978-1-5081-4196-9 (pbk.)
ISBN 978-1-5081-4197-6 (6-pack)
ISBN 978-1-5081-4198-3 (library binding)
1. Capitals (Cities) — United States — Juvenile literature. 2. Cities and towns — United States — Juvenile literature. I. Title.
E180.B43 2016
973—d23

Manufactured in the United States of America

CPSIA Compliance Information: Batch #BW16PK: For Further Information contact Rosen Publishing, New York, New York at 1-800-237-9932

Contents

We live in a state capital.

6

A state capital is a city or town. This means it is an urban community.

A state capital is where
a state's leaders work.

9

The leaders of a state make laws. Laws are important rules.

The governor is the head
of our state.

14

Our state's leaders meet in one building in our city. It is called the **capitol**.

There is a **museum** in our city. It has things to look at from our state's past.

Every state has its own capital.

There are 50 state capitals in the United States.

WASHINGTON

OREGON

MONTANA

NORTH DAKOTA

MINNESOTA

MAINE

IDAHO

SOUTH DAKOTA

WISCONSIN

MICHIGAN

N.H
VT.
NEW YORK
MASS.
R.I.
CONN.

WYOMING

NEBRASKA

IOWA

PENNSYLVANIA

NEW JERSEY

NEVADA

UTAH

COLORADO

ILLINOIS

INDIANA

OHIO

DELAWARE
WASHINGTON DC

WEST VIRGINIA

CALIFORNIA

KANSAS

MISSOURI

KENTUCKY

VIRGINIA

ARIZONA

OKLAHOMA

ARKANSAS

TENNESSEE

NORTH CAROLINA

NEW MEXICO

MISSISSIPPI

MONTGOMERY

GEORGIA

SOUTH CAROLINA

TEXAS

LOUISIANA

FLORIDA

ALASKA

HAWAII

★ = state capital

21

It is fun to live in such an important city.

23

Words to Know

capitol

museum

Index

Websites

Due to the changing nature of Internet links, PowerKids Press has developed an online list of websites related to the subject of this book. This site is updated regularly. Please use this link to access the list: www.powerkidslinks.com/acom/stcap